W9-AXE-496

 little bee books

An imprint of Bonnier Publishing USA
251 Park Avenue South, New York, NY 10010
Copyright © 2017 by Bonnier Publishing USA
All rights reserved, including the right of reproduction in whole or in part in any form.
LITTLE BEE BOOKS is a trademark of Bonnier Publishing USA, and associated colophon is a trademark of Bonnier Publishing USA.
Manufactured in the United States   LB 0517
First Edition   10 9 8 7 6 5 4 3 2 1

Library of Congress Cataloging-in-Publication Data:
Names: Ohlin, Nancy, author. | Simó, Roger, illustrator
Title: The Salem Witch Trials / Nancy Ohlin; illustrated by Roger Simó.
Description: New York: little bee books, 2017. | Series: Blast Back!
Subjects: LCSH: Trials (Witchcraft)—Massachusetts—Salem—Juvenile literature. | Witchcraft—Massachusetts—Salem—History—Juvenile literature. | Salem (Mass.)—History—Colonial period, ca. 1600-1775—Juvenile literature. | BISAC: JUVENILE NONFICTION / History / United States / Colonial & Revolutionary Periods. | JUVENILE NONFICTION / People & Places / United States / General. | JUVENILE NONFICTION / Social Science / Sociology. | Classification: LCC KFM2478.8.W5 O55 2017
DDC 133.4/3097445—dc23 | LC record available at https://lccn.loc.gov/2017004951

Identifiers: LCCN 2017004951
ISBN 978-1-4998-0450-8 (pbk) | ISBN 978-1-4998-0451-5 (hc)

littlebeebooks.com
bonnierpublishingusa.com

BLAST BACK!

THE SALEM WITCH TRIALS

by Nancy Ohlin   illustrated by Roger Simó

little bee books

CONTENTS

CANADA

MASSACHUSETTS
BAY COLONY

SALEM VILLAGE

BOSTON

Introduction

Have you ever heard people mention the Salem witch trials and wondered what they were talking about? Were actual witches on trial? What were their crimes? Were they found innocent or guilty? And what are witches, anyway?

Let's blast back in time for a little adventure and find out. . . .

A Brief History of the Salem Witch Trials

In 1692, residents of Salem Village in the Massachusetts Bay Colony began accusing people of being possessed by the devil and practicing witchcraft. (Back then, Massachusetts was a colony; it was not a state until 1788.)

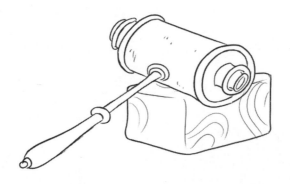

The governor of Massachusetts set up a special court to try the accused. "Try" means to figure out if a person is innocent or guilty of a crime through a process called a trial. Between June and September of 1692, the special court tried and found twenty of the accused to be guilty. All twenty were sentenced to death. A sentence is a punishment that is given to a criminal at the end of a trial.

In October of 1692, the governor of Massachusetts shut down the special court and set up a *different* court to continue trying more of the accused. In May of 1693, he shut down this court, too, because public sentiment had shifted against the trials. He freed all the remaining prisoners.

By the end, around 200 people (men as well as women) had been accused and imprisoned. Twenty were executed and others died while in prison.

What Are Witches?

When you think about witches, you probably picture a scary-looking old woman wearing a black cape and pointy hat and riding a broom across the sky. But that image isn't really based in fact—it's more about cartoons and Halloween costumes.

Still, the idea of witches is quite real. Different cultures throughout history have held different concepts of witches and witchcraft. Generally speaking, witches are people (usually women) who are believed to have magical abilities. Witchcraft is the type of magic they practice.

But what is "magic"? In present-day Western civilization, magic is commonly thought to be pure illusion (something that seems real, but isn't), trickery (an act meant to confuse or deceive), or sleight of hand (a kind of trick that involves moving the hands around quickly so the viewer can't see what exactly is happening). In the past, however, many believed people could have magical powers and

supernatural abilities; they believed in the existence of witches, wizards, and/or sorcerers. (Sorcerers are magicians who are thought to get their powers from evil spirits and/or practice magic for evil purposes.) Even today, there are individuals, religious groups, social groups, and cultures that believe in some type of magic.

Examples of Witchcraft

Spells: spoken or unspoken words intended to cause a magical effect such as healing, harming, protecting, etc.

Potions: mixtures of herbs and other ingredients intended to do the same

Divination: predicting the future or discovering information about the unknown by means of magic

Astrology: divination that uses the moon, sun, and other celestial bodies

Alchemy: turning lead, copper, or other common metal into gold or silver or into an elixir of immortality

Necromancy: communicating with the dead

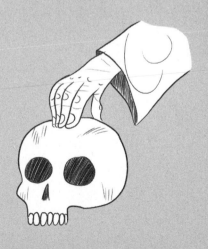

Wicca

Today, there exists a contemporary witchcraft movement called Wicca. Followed mostly in the Western world, Wicca includes the worship of a female deity (the Goddess) and other deities (such as the Horned God), the honoring of nature, and the practice of magic (usually in the form of rituals that help Wiccans connect with the divine). Wiccans celebrate Halloween, the spring equinox (a solar event that happens around the first day of spring), the summer solstice (the beginning of summer), and other special events.

23

Witch Hunts in Europe

The Salem witch trials weren't the first witch trials in history, and they weren't the last, either. From the early fourteenth to the late eighteenth century, approximately 110,000 witches in Europe were accused and tried. Between 40,000 and 60,000 of them are believed to have been put to death.

As with the Salem witch trials, these events in Europe are sometimes referred to as "witch hunts" because people were aggressively searching for witches in their midst. These witches were thought to be followers of the devil who used magic for evil, associated with demons, could shape-shift into animals or other humans, rode through the air to secret witch gatherings, had "familiars," and so on. (A familiar is a witch's demonic servant or companion in animal form.)

Most experts agree that there have been devil worshipers throughout history. However, none of these devil worshipers ever shape-shifted, rode through the air, or did any of the other things witches were accused of doing.

The witch hunts in Europe (and elsewhere) were often fueled by rumor, gossip, and prejudice rather than logic and physical evidence. For example, a townswoman might be accused of witchcraft because she could cure illnesses with herbs, or because she was very attached to her pet cat—because it must be her familiar! Mass hysteria was another big part of the witch hunts. (Mass hysteria happens when a large group of people have wild, irrational outbursts of fear and emotion centered upon a common theme or belief.)

"Witch Finder Generall"

In seventeenth-century England, a lawyer named Matthew Hopkins became a "Witch Finder Generall" (or Witchfinder General) when he went into the business of hunting witches for a fee. He traveled to towns and villages and convinced local residents to hire him and his assistants to find witches. He'd then get these alleged witches to confess and see to it that they were hanged by the authorities. Hopkins and his team managed to round up more than 230 "witches" and made a great deal of money.

Hopkins's methods for proving that a person was guilty of practicing witchcraft ranged from the ridiculous to the cruel. For example, he would tie an accused witch to a chair and wait patiently. If a mouse or fly or similar creature appeared in the room, Hopkins would declare the animal to be the witch's familiar. Hopkins would also stick long pins into the accused's body to see if he or she had

"witch's marks." (Witch's marks are basically just moles or warts that are said to supply the witch's familiar with blood to feed upon.)

Witch Hunts in the American Colonies

In the seventeenth century, there was no United States of America yet. What we call the U.S. today was a collection of colonies that had been formed by settlers from Britain and other countries.

The American colonies had their share of witch hunts before Salem—for example, in the colony of Connecticut. In 1642, the Connecticut government decided that witchcraft was a capital crime. (A capital crime is one that is punishable by death.) In 1647 in Hartford, Connecticut, Alse (Alice) Young became the first accused witch to be executed in the American colonies. At least nine other Connecticut "witches" were put to death over the next fifteen years.

The colonists' feelings about witches and witchcraft were strongly influenced by Puritanism. Puritans were Protestant Christians who came over from Britain to settle in the colonies; they were very strict about religious matters. They believed that the devil roamed the earth in order to tempt humans into doing his evil deeds. Furthermore, they believed that witches were servants of the devil.

There are passages in the Bible about witches. One of them, from the Book of Leviticus, reads: "A man also or a woman that hath a familiar spirit, or that is a wizard, shall surely be put to death." Another passage, this time from the Book of Exodus, reads: "Thou shalt not suffer a witch to live."

MASSACHUSETTS
BAY COLONY

Some, but not all, of the villagers wanted independence from the town. This deepened the divide between town and village and also created

PLYMOUTH COLONY

Salem Town and
Salem Village

One of the first colonies in America was the Massachusetts Bay Colony. It had been settled in 1630 by approximately one thousand Puritans from England. By the mid-1640s, its population had grown to over 20,000.

In the late 1600s, Salem was actually different places in the Massachusetts Bay Col Salem Town and Salem Village. Salem Town w busy commercial port on Massachusetts Bay. Sa Village was a farming community about ten m inland that was controlled by (and was considere part of) Salem Town.

36

37

PLYMOUTH
COLONY

Salem Town and Salem Village

One of the first colonies in America was the Massachusetts Bay Colony. It had been settled in 1630 by approximately one thousand Puritans from England. By the mid-1640s, its population had grown to over 20,000.

In the late 1600s, Salem was actually two different places in the Massachusetts Bay Colony: Salem Town and Salem Village. Salem Town was a busy commercial port on Massachusetts Bay. Salem Village was a farming community about ten miles inland that was controlled by (and was considered a part of) Salem Town.

Some, but not all, of the villagers wanted independence from the town. This deepened the divide between town and village and also created

"battle lines" among the villagers—those who wanted independence versus those who were against independence.

Two families came to represent the two sides: the Porters and the Putnams. The Porters were big landowners in the village but had close ties to the rich merchants in Salem Town and were also involved in the government there. The Porters were opposed to independence. The Putnams, too, were big landowners in the village. However, they

considered themselves to be simple farmers with traditional Puritan values, and they did not approve of the wealthy townspeople who seemed to look out only for themselves rather than the community at large. The Putnams were in favor of independence.

The rivalry between the Putnams and the Porters set the stage for the Salem witch trials.

Reverend Parris

In 1689, the Putnams used their power and steady influence to get a new pastor for the Congregational church in Salem Village, which had been founded in 1672. The new pastor's name was Samuel Parris.

Reverend Parris was a Boston merchant who had wanted to change careers from being a businessman to a minister. (The terms "minister," "pastor," and "reverend" all mean the same thing here.) Before residing in Boston, he had lived on the Caribbean island of Barbados, where he owned a sugar plantation. (Back then, Barbados was a British colony.) He had studied religion at Harvard College (now Harvard University).

Reverend Parris moved from Boston to Salem Village with his wife, two children, a niece, and two slaves he had brought to Boston from Barbados: John Indian and a woman named Tituba.

The Congregational church was not an easy place to be a minister. Both Salem Town and Salem Village residents attended the church and brought with them their disagreements and other conflicts.

Reverend Parris didn't make things any easier. As the fourth pastor of the church, he rubbed some people the wrong way with his demands for higher pay, his old-fashioned brand of Puritanism, and his strict rules about non-members of the church. (For example, he insisted that non-members leave the church before an important part of the service called "communion.")

Strange Behavior

In January of 1692, Parris's nine-year-old daughter Elizabeth (called Betty), his eleven-year-old niece Abigail Williams, and their twelve-year-old friend Ann Putnam, Jr. started doing some playful "fortune-telling." (Fortune-telling was considered witchcraft and not appropriate for Puritans.) Then Betty and Abigail began exhibiting strange behavior. They had fits, threw things, screamed, and twisted and contorted their bodies. They also complained of physical sensations that felt as though they were being pinched and bitten. (Ann would display the same strange behavior much later on.)

The local doctor, William Griggs, could not come up with a medical explanation for all this. In February, he declared that the cause must be supernatural.

Dr. Griggs's "diagnosis" caught on. A neighbor suggested to Tituba that she bake a "witch cake" to figure out what magical forces were responsible for the girls' condition.

Reverend Parris was furious at Tituba for making the witch cake. He considered it to be a blasphemous act that was greatly disrespectful to God.

What Is Voodoo?

The girls' interest in fortune-telling may have been inspired by Tituba and her stories about voodoo. Voodoo is a religion with roots in Africa. Slaves brought it over to the Caribbean, where it mingled with Christian ideas. Those who practice voodoo believe in both a Christian god and different kinds of spirits. They pray to (and perform rites for) God and certain spirits in exchange for health, protection, and other positive benefits. Connection with the spiritual realm is an important aspect of voodoo.

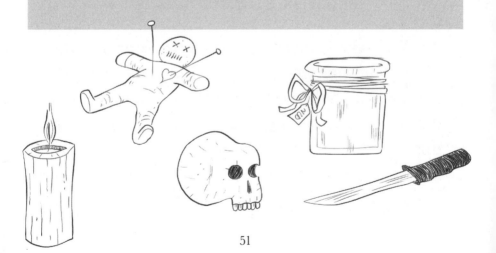

What *Really* Caused Those Symptoms?

Modern-day experts have speculated on what might have triggered the fits, seizures, and other strange behavior of Betty and Abigail. Theories include child abuse, Lyme disease, epilepsy (a brain disorder that causes convulsions), asthma (a condition that makes it hard to breathe), encephalitis (an inflammation of the brain), delusional psychosis (a type of mental illness where a person can't tell the difference between what's real and what's not), and also a disease called convulsive ergotism, which results from eating bread, cereal, or other grain-based food infected with a fungus called ergot. One historian, however, chalked up the girls' strange behavior to juvenile delinquency (which means young people misbehaving and committing crimes).

Three "Witches"

Reverend Parris pressured Betty and Abigail to name the person or persons who had caused their condition. The girls confessed that Tituba and two other local women, Sarah Good and Sarah Osborn, had bewitched them. Good and Osborn were not regular churchgoers or prominent members of the community. Good was a bad-tempered beggar and Osborn was an old, bedridden woman.

On March 1, 1692, two magistrates (or officials) from Salem Town came to Salem Village to set up a public inquiry into the matter. This inquiry consisted of a series of informal hearings; there were no actual trials.

At the beginning of the inquiry, all three accused women said they were innocent; however, Sarah Good accused Sarah Osborn of being a witch. After being questioned repeatedly by the magistrates, beaten, and no doubt feeling powerless because she was a slave, Tituba changed her story and gave the men the confession they had been waiting for: that she had been visited by the devil and had made a deal with him, and that she had seen Good's and Osborn's names in the so-called "devil's book." (Tituba said there were seven other names in the book that she had not been able to make out.)

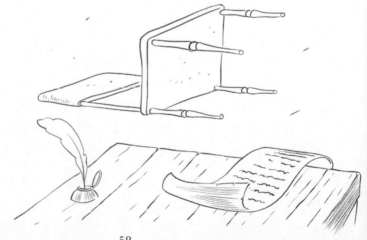

The Hysteria Grows

With Tituba's confession, as well as Sarah Good's accusation against Sarah Osborn, the magistrates believed that they had proof of the existence of witches in Salem—not just Good, Osborn, and Tituba, but the other names listed in the devil's book.

Mass hysteria erupted. The Puritanical citizens of Salem panicked at the thought that there might be witches—the devil's servants—among them spreading evil.

Other girls and women in the community claimed to experience fits, seizures, and other bizarre symptoms, too, including Ann Putnam, Jr. (Betty and Abigail's friend), Ann's mother, Ann's cousin Mary Walcott, and Mercy Lewis, who was a servant of the Putnam family. They then accused *other* girls and women in the community of being the witches responsible for their mysterious sickness.

And it wasn't just poor or powerless people who were being charged; others were accused as well, including a seventy-one-year-old grandmother and well-respected citizen named Rebecca Nurse and her sister, Mary Easty, who had seven children and was known for her kindness and religious spirit.

As the weeks wore on, members of the Putnam family and their friends seemed to be doing most of the accusing, and many of the accused seemed to be enemies of the Putnams, like those with connections to the Porter family.

Many of these alleged "witches" were put in prison to await trial.

The Youngest Witch

Dorothy "Dorcas" Good, the four-year-old daughter of Sarah Good, was accused of witchcraft along with her mother. Jailed at age five, she became the youngest person to be imprisoned during the trials. (She was released eight and a half months later.)

The Court of Oyer and Terminer

On May 27, 1692, the governor of Massachusetts Bay Colony, Sir William Phips, stepped in and ordered a court to be set up in Salem Town to try the accused. The court was called the Court of Oyer (an old legal term that means "to hear") and Terminer (a similar term that means "to decide").

The lieutenant governor, William Stoughton, was in charge of the court, which had seven judges. The accused (also called "defendants") had to defend themselves on the witness stand without lawyers to assist them.

At times when a defendant was testifying about his or her own innocence, people in the audience would start writhing and moaning and whimpering as though the defendant was a witch casting dark magic over them. And some of the defendants turned on other defendants, accusing them of witchcraft in the hope of gaining favor with the judges.

Those who would not confess to being guilty were sentenced to death. If a defendant confessed, she or he was spared according to the Puritan idea that it was God's place to punish the guilty. No one who confessed was convicted or executed. But those who confessed suffered in other ways. They were ostracized—or rejected—by the community. Their families fell into financial ruin.

There were many in Salem (and elsewhere) who thought that the trials were terribly unfair and not based upon factual evidence at all. There was no actual proof that the accused were witches, only a lot

of finger-pointing and wild stories. But people were afraid to speak up in case they, too, might be accused of witchcraft and then arrested.

The Accusations

The citizens of Salem accused the defendants of all sorts of bizarre things, including:

- Turning into a cat and flying out a window
- Bringing bad weather
- Ruining crops
- Sending spirits to attack them
- Inflicting sickness on their livestock
- Signing a contract with the devil
- Making cheese spoil

Cotton Mather

Cotton Mather (1663–1728) was a famous New England Puritan and American Congregational minister who lived in the town of Boston in the Massachusetts Bay Colony. He believed in both witchcraft and science. The author of over 400 books, he published a book in 1689 called *Memorable Providences Relating to Witchcraft and Possessions*.... In the book, he described the strange behavior (similar to Betty Parris's and Abigail Williams's) of some siblings in Boston who were thought to have been bewitched.

Cotton believed those who practiced magic for evil should be punished, so he was very much in favor of the Salem witch trials.

That being said, he (along with his father, Increase Mather, who was also a minister) tried to convince the trial judges to disregard "spectral evidence." Spectral evidence is testimony given by a person who claims to have been attacked by a specter, or spirit, who looked just like someone the victim knows. For example, when seventy-one-year-old Rebecca Nurse was found innocent of her charges, the girls who had accused her of witchcraft started to shout in the courtroom that Nurse's ghost was attacking them and trying to kill them right then and there. As a result, the judges changed Nurse's verdict to "guilty."

The Verdicts

On June 2, 1692, an innkeeper named Bridget Bishop became the first defendant to be convicted, or found guilty. On June 10, she was hanged in Salem Village on a hill that came to be called Gallows Hill. ("Gallows" refers to death by hanging.)

Five more defendants were hanged on July 19, including Sarah Good and Rebecca Nurse.

On August 19, another five defendants were hanged. One of them was George Burroughs, who was one of the pastors of the Congregational church before Reverend Parris. Burroughs had moved to Maine after leaving his position at the church. But he was brought back to Salem, accused of being an organizer of witches, and found guilty.

Eight more defendants were hanged on September 22. The husband of one of the defendants, Giles Corey, was also accused of witchcraft. A man in his eighties, he refused to plead guilty or innocent. He was executed by being pressed under heavy stones for two days until he died.

As the trials went on, people in other Massachusetts communities—like Beverly, Andover, Charlestown, Lynn, and Marblehead—were accused of witchcraft, too. The hysteria was spreading well beyond Salem.

Canine Witches?

Humans weren't the only ones who were executed during this period. In October of 1692, a girl in the town of Andover, Massachusetts, claimed that a neighbor's dog had bewitched her. The poor dog was shot by the townspeople, then later declared "innocent" by Cotton Mather. (He said the dog, which survived the bullets, would have died if it had been truly guilty.) In Salem Village, some girls accused a man named John Bradstreet of bewitching a dog. Bradstreet fled to another colony before he was formally accused, and the dog was hanged as a witch.

I Object!

Judge Nathaniel Saltonstall, who was one of the judges during the trials, resigned from the Court of Oyer and Terminer after the trial of Bridget Bishop. He didn't believe that Bishop or any of the other defendants were guilty, and he objected to the weight given to all the spectral evidence.

New Court, New Trials

On October 29, the governor of Massachusetts Bay Colony, Sir William Phips, stopped the trials being conducted by the Court of Oyer and Terminer. One reason may have been the fact that his own wife had been accused of witchcraft. In its place, he established a new court, the Superior Court of Judicature, which was to set a higher standard for evidence (including not admitting spectral testimony).

New trials resumed in January and February of 1693. Fifty-six people were tried, but only three were convicted. No one was executed.

By May of 1693, the trials came to an end. The witch hunt hysteria had ebbed. The public was no longer afraid to speak out against the trials. There was great concern that innocent people were being imprisoned and executed. There was also no real evidence against the accused. Governor Phips pardoned the three who had been convicted and released anyone still in custody.

Samuel Sewall

Born in England in 1652, Samuel Sewall was a British-American colonial merchant and judge. His family moved to Massachusetts Bay Colony when he was a boy, and he later graduated from Harvard College. Appointed to the Court of Oyer and Terminer by Governor Phips, he was the only judge to declare that the Salem witch trials had been wrong. He wrote a confession to that effect, and his minister read the confession out loud at the Old South Church in Boston with Sewall in attendance.

Sewall went on to become the Chief Justice of the Superior Court of Judicature in Massachusetts. He also authored many works including *The Selling of Joseph* (1700), which argued against slavery, and *A Memorial Related to the Kennebeck Indians* (1721), which argued against the inhumane treatment of Native Americans. He died in Boston in 1730.

Whatever Happened to Tituba?

The courts did not sentence Tituba to death because she had "confessed." She did, however, spend fifteen long months in jail. Eventually released, she may have been sold to a new slave owner in exchange for payment of her jail fees. After that, there is no historical record of her.

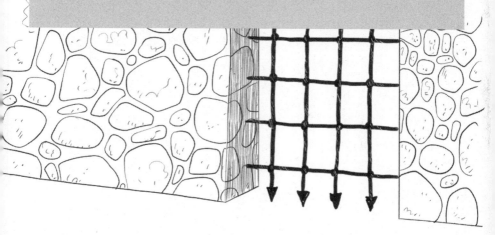

The "Witch of Pungo"

The Salem witch trials were not the last witch hunts in North America. In 1698, a woman named Grace Sherwood who lived in Pungo, Virginia, was accused by a neighbor of witchcraft. (The neighbor said that Sherwood had transformed into a black cat and attacked her.) Sherwood was not arrested or convicted. But she wasn't so lucky when she was accused of witchcraft by another neighbor in 1706. She was given a "witch's ducking." With a witch's ducking, the accused was plunged into deep water to determine guilt or innocence. If the accused floated, it meant she was guilty. If she drowned, it meant she was innocent (but would die by drowning). Sherwood was tied up with rope and thrown off a boat into the Lynnhaven River. She managed somehow to untie herself and float to the surface, which meant that she was guilty. She spent seven years in prison.

The Legacy of the Trials

In January of 1697, the General Court of Massachusetts declared a day of contemplation (or thinking deeply) and fasting (not eating or drinking) to remember the tragic outcome of the trials.

Also in January, one of the Salem witch trial judges, Samuel Sewall, confessed that the trials had been a mistake. He was the only judge to admit to this.

In 1702, the General Court of Massachusetts declared that the trials had been illegal.

Ann Putnam, Jr. apologized in 1706 for her role as one of the accusers, saying, "Now I have just grounds and good reason to believe they were innocent persons."

In 1711, the Commonwealth of Massachusetts exonerated (or released from blame) twenty-two of the thirty-three defendants who had been convicted. (The other eleven were not exonerated by the state of Massachusetts until 2001.)

In 1957, the state of Massachusetts made a formal apology for the trials.

The terrible mistakes and abuses of law that had occurred during the Salem witch trials inspired positive reforms in legal proceedings—for example, considering a defendant to be innocent until proven guilty, a defendant's right to be represented by a lawyer, and a defendant's right to cross-examine (or question on the witness stand) one's accuser.

The Communist Witch Hunts

The term "witch hunt" is often used to describe a movement that occured in the United States in the 1950s. At that time, America considered the Soviet Union to be its biggest enemy, and Communism was the political philosophy of the Soviets. A U.S. senator named Joseph McCarthy led the efforts to weed out any Communists who lived in the country. Thousands were accused of being Communist sympathizers. Many were coerced into testifying against their friends and colleagues—just like in the Salem witch trials.

"McCarthyism" is a term that means accusing people of treason and other crimes without proper evidence.

The Crucible

The Crucible is a 1953 play by playwright Arthur Miller. It is a fictionalized drama based on the real-life people and events of the Salem witch trials. It is also an allegory of the McCarthy era. (An allegory is a story with a hidden meaning that is often moral or political.) Widely regarded as one of the most important plays in the history of theater, *The Crucible* was first performed in New York City and was also adapted for film, TV, and opera. (The opera adaptation won the Pulitzer Prize for Music in 1962.)

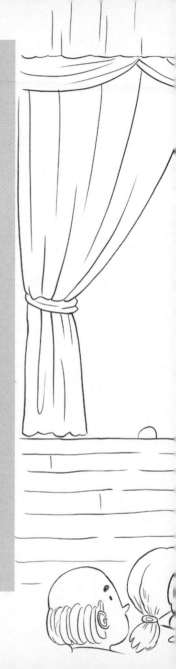

Whatever Happened to
Salem Town and Salem Village?

Today, Salem Town is the city of Salem, Massachusetts. Salem Village is the town of Danvers, Massachusetts. In Danvers, you can visit the Witchcraft Victims' Memorial, the site of the Salem Village Parsonage (where the Parris family lived, and before them, Reverend George Burroughs, who was dragged back from Maine and hanged for witchcraft), and other places of historical interest. In Salem, you can visit the Salem Witch Museum, the Salem Witch Trials Memorial, and other sites.

Well, it's been a great adventure. Good-bye, Salem witch trials!

Where to next?

Also available:

ANCIENT EGYPT
by Nancy Ohlin
Illustrated by Adam Larkum

ANCIENT GREECE
by Nancy Ohlin
Illustrated by Adam Larkum

THE AMERICAN REVOLUTION
by Nancy Ohlin
Illustrated by Adam Larkum

THE CIVIL WAR
by Nancy Ohlin
Illustrated by Adam Larkum

THE TITANIC
by Nancy Ohlin
Illustrated by Adam Larkum

WORLD WAR II
by Nancy Ohlin
Illustrated by Roger Simó

VIKINGS
by Nancy Ohlin
Illustrated by Adam Larkum

THE GREAT WALL OF CHINA
by Nancy Ohlin
Illustrated by Adam Larkum

Selected Bibliography

"A Brief History of the Salem Witch Trials," *Smithsonian* magazine online, http://www.smithsonianmag.com/history/a-brief-history-of-the-salem-witch-trials-175162489/?no-ist

"Animals in the Salem Witch Trials" by Rebecca Beatrice Brooks, http://historyofmassachusetts.org/animals-in-the-salem-witch-trials/

"Before Salem, the First American Witch Hunt," *History* magazine online,

http://www.history.com/news/before-salem-the-first-american-witch-hunt

Encyclopedia Britannica Kids Online, kids.britannica.com

Encyclopedia Britannica Online, www.britannica.com

"Grace Sherwood: The Witch of Pungo," Virginia Historical Society online, http://www.vahistorical.org/collections-and-resources/virginia-history-explorer/grace-sherwood-witch-pungo

The Salem Witch Trials by Don Nardo, Lucent Books, 2007

"The Witches of Salem" by Stacey Schiff, *The New Yorker*, September 7, 2015

NANCY OHLIN is the author of the YA novels *Always, Forever* and *Beauty* as well as the early chapter book series Greetings from Somewhere under the pseudonym Harper Paris. She lives in Ithaca, New York, with her husband, their two kids, four cats, and assorted animals who happen to show up at their door. Visit her online at nancyohlin.com.

ROGER SIMÓ is an illustrator based in a town near Barcelona, where he lives with his wife, son, and daughter. He has become the person that he would have envied when he was a child: someone who makes a living by drawing and explaining fantastic stories.